BRITAIN IN PICTURES
THE BRITISH PEOPLE IN PICTURES

ROMAN BRITAIN

The Editor is most grateful to all those who have
so kindly helped in the selection of illustrations
especially to officials of the various public
Museums Libraries and Galleries and
to all others who have generously
allowed pictures and MSS
to be reproduced

ROMAN BRITAIN

IAN RICHMOND

WITH
8 PLATES IN COLOUR
AND
22 ILLUSTRATIONS IN
BLACK & WHITE

BRACKEN BOOKS
LONDON

First published 1947
This edition published 1987 by Bracken Books
a division of Bestseller Publications Ltd
Princess House, 50 Eastcastle Street
London W1

ISBN 1 85170 116 8

Printed and bound in Great Britain
by Collins, Glasgow

LIST OF ILLUSTRATIONS

PLATES IN COLOUR

BLACK AND WHITE ILLUSTRATIONS

HEAD OF A BRITON, IN BRONZE
Second century A.D.
Mounting from a bucket, Brough on Humber

THE CONQUEST

THE outstanding difference between the Roman and earlier periods
of British history is that the Roman age furnishes the first surviving
comment upon the scene. From then onwards written and material
evidence corroborate and enhance one another. It is, for example, a Roman
writer who observes that lack of unity among the natives was the most
potent factor in Rome's success ; while archaeology attests that the disunity
of Britain at the time of the Roman conquest was profound and widespread. As has been explained in an earlier volume of this series (*Early
Britain*), the island had already absorbed many invaders, and when the
Romans first reached it, in 55 B.C., the different groups had not yet settled
down. The best illustration of the chaos is that when Julius Caesar most
needed intelligence concerning the interior he was unable to obtain it,
owing to the cleavage between the recently-arrived Belgic conquerors of
the South-East and the indigenous peoples. Nor did the difference grow
less sharp during the century which elapsed before the invasion of Claudius
in A.D. 43. By that time the newcomers had increased, both in numbers
and aggressiveness.

In the South-East, in an area roughly corresponding to Hertfordshire
and Essex, with allied or subject tribes south of the Thames, lay
the rapidly-expanding Belgic kingdom of the Catuvellauni, whose king

7

Cunobellinus (Shakespeare's Cymbeline) had conquered and subjected the Trinovantes. In the South, covering respectively Hampshire, Dorsetshire and Wiltshire together with much of Somersetshire, lay the Atrebates, the Durotriges and the Belgae, almost all newcomers since Caesar's day and mostly fugitives from his wrath. There is no reason to expect unity among these predatory and warlike communities, and it is even more certain that there was none among the inland folk who were their victims. These older tribes were the Parisi of East Yorkshire, the Iceni of Norfolk and Suffolk, the Coritani of Lincolnshire and Leicestershire, the Dobunni of the Cotswolds and the Dumnonii of Devon and Cornwall. And beyond them lay the diverse hill-men of Wales and the loosely-knit Brigantes, as the dalesfolk of the Pennines were called. These are the first tribes in British history to which names can be attached, and their diversity and antagonism rendered the age indeed an Iron Age. The newest arrivals were merciless, broken men who had all to gain and nothing to lose by ruthlessness. Their headquarters were hill-fortresses of immense strength, refuges against the chronic inter-tribal forays, marked by head-hunting, wholesale pillage and enslavement. In self-defence, the inland folk imitated at least these precautions. The ascendant elements in society were everywhere the aristocratic warriors with bands of followers, sometimes compared with Homeric chieftains of Greece. It was a vainglorious epoch, an age of sagas and decorative art focused upon the individual. So polished indeed is the art as to suggest a leisure and tranquillity which all other evidence belies. The concentrated brilliance which illumines this age of darkness does not make it an age of light.

Politically, it was no satisfaction to the Roman government across the Channel to have virtually within sight so turbulent a world. The wild freedom of Britain was a perpetual incitement. It offered a fresh start to renegade chieftains who, like the king of the Gallic Atrebates, could not bear the sight of a Roman. It was a ready refuge to fugitives from Roman executive power. This does not mean that British chiefs were reluctant to enter into relations with Rome. There was much interchange, economic and political, from the time of Augustus onwards, and the reason for it was the lure of Roman material civilisation. Princely burial chambers, stocked with offerings to the dead, give a picture of the wines and rich table furnishings which left the Roman world to enliven the feasts of paramount chiefs: and in exchange, chained neck to neck in iron collars, came slaves, sometimes at the pitiless rate of one slave per jar of wine, to fill the expanding Roman labour market. The traffic was doubtless welcome to the principals of both sides. It furnished a pretty penny in Imperial duties at the Gallic ports, while in Britain the Roman merchandise certainly reached important households of the lowlands, as far north as Leicestershire and as far west as Somersetshire. A bold and florid native coinage, in gold and silver, tells of imitation also. The pieces themselves,

8

related in weight and sizes to standards derived from the Greek, went to Rome for their design : their lettering was Roman, their language Latin and their production often due to Roman moneyers. It was this peaceful penetration that helped the Roman army staff to appreciate the situation in Britain and plan the annexation under Claudius. But the actual circumstances of acquisition were the product of no set plan.

In A.D. 40 the aged Cunobellinus expelled his son Adminius, who fled and did unconditional homage to the Emperor Gaius, at the moment when at least a demonstration against Britain was being planned. Before three years had elapsed, the king was dead and his two other sons, Caratacus and Togodumnus, had divided the inheritance. Then, in A.D. 43, another chieftain from south of the Thames sought safety from insurrection at the court of Claudius. Requests for extradition of the exiles were refused and raids upon Roman territory followed. Politically, the moment had thus arrived to teach the Britons a lesson. But personal ambition also played a part upon the Roman side. The new Emperor Claudius, unexpectedly supreme after long retirement, itched to gratify his suppressed ambitions and family pride by a triumphant novel conquest. Thus, inevitable though the ultimate annexation of Britain may seem on the longer view, the immediate causes were not impersonal. On the British side they amply confirm the broad conclusion of Tacitus that British disunity was Rome's best asset.

A large force of five legions and corresponding auxiliary troops was used, commanded by able generals of wide experience in frontier warfare, and there is no mistaking their objectives. The first campaign was swiftly directed against the confederacy of Caratacus and Togodumnus. It met with no opposition upon landing, but the Medway crossing was severely contested and considerable effort was needed to establish a bridgehead on the Thames Here came a pause, while Claudius himself arrived for a fortnight's campaigning against Camulodunum (Colchester). The second campaign followed the Emperor's departure and was directed against the Belgic tribes of the South-West whose hill-fortresses had to be stormed one by one. Such a *Blitzkrieg* was a heavy effort, but the heavy-armed legionaries, skilled in siege-craft, could take it in their stride. The commander on this front was the hard-headed future Emperor Vespasian, whose reputation was thus made.

Onlookers regarded the results as decisive. All the great inland communities, long terrorised by the tribes now defeated, arranged alliances with Rome. Thus, without further effort, the Roman armies could move forward to the Humber and the Severn, basing themselves upon a solid block of unravaged allied territory and soon disposing of resources in commissariat and tribute under treaty terms now rapidly settled by plenipotentiaries on the spot. If this achievement was not foreseen by those who planned the campaigns, it must have been recognised as the reward of operations which had exploited British disunity to the full.

Roman suzerainty was thus freely accepted by the older-established tribes and, once accepted, was legally ratified. But there was a price to pay for peace ensured by Rome. "Peace," as a famous Roman commander-in-chief remarked, "has to be fought for ; fighters need pay ; and pay demands tribute." In these matters the duties of the allied and subject communities would differ in degree rather than kind. There was the Roman army of occupation to be fed by an annual tribute of corn for bread and hogs for lard. The Roman military engineers were to be assisted by requisitioned drafts of unskilled labour. There was tribute in money for provincial taxation, direct and indirect, in men for the Roman auxiliary army, and in beasts for mounts, haulage and hides. These demands would fall heavily upon folk unused to regular contributions of the kind and the guarantors for the fulfilment were the tribal aristocrats.

A no less heavy price was paid for the new civilisation. Roman fashions in housing and clothing and other items of material comfort became *de rigueur* for the upper classes. Personal vanity, ambition, rivalry, desire to stand well with Rome and genuine interest in Roman culture ensured this result, apart from Roman pressure. Presently, in the new provincial capital founded at Camulodunum, there were festivals and priesthoods in Roman fashion and ritual to be filled in turn. Economically and psychologically, the impact of the new civilisation was thus exceptionally severe, and in Southern Britain the full impact was soon felt, owing to the speed of the conquest and the friendliness of many communities.

One of the friendliest groups was the *Regnenses*, as the Sussex folk of the kingdom (*regnum*) of Cogidumnus were called. This king received Roman citizenship and was actually given rule over other communities as well as his own, with the novel title of "King and Imperial legate in Britain." His policy of Romanisation is attested by two remarkable inscriptions. A marble tablet describes in Latin, couched in formal legal phrasing, the erection on donated land of a temple to Neptune and Minerva for a guild of smiths. The second stone, now lost, was a loyal dedication to the Emperor Nero, whose lineage was set out as fully as in Rome. This kind of communal urbanity represents high attainment in Roman ways, not outclassed by any other Western province in its early stages.

Resistance, however, there was, in sharp reaction to the friends of Rome. Active warfare was for some time concentrated in Wales. Thither went Caratacus, to become leader of resistance among the Silures of Monmouthshire and the Ordovices of Powys until his crushing defeat in 51 : after which he fled to the Brigantes, whose alliance with Rome defeated his hopes and led to his delivery in chains to adorn the triumph of Claudius. The triumph once over, Claudius, with rare magnanimity, pardoned him and restored him to his captured wife and family. But the fire which Caratacus had kindled was harder to quench. Fierce guerilla warfare lasted a generation longer. Minor revolts also began among the allies. As it became

English Equivalents
of Roman Place Names

1	Exeter	13	St Albans
2	Dorchester	14	Colchester
3	Chichester	15	Kenchester
4	Winchester	16	Wroxeter
5	Canterbury	17	Leicester
6	Silchester	18	Caister
7	Bath	19	Lincoln
8	Caerleon	20	Chester
9	Caerwent	21	Brough
10	Gloucester	22	York
11	Cirencester	23	Aldborough
12	London	24	Inchtuthill

0   100

Scale of Miles

• Towns
○ Townships
■ Fortresses
▪ Forts
～ Frontier Wall
✕ Mines

MAP OF ROMAN BRITAIN

evident that the Roman armies had enveloped them for good and all, first the Iceni and then others rose in protest, and these clouds of unrest burst with terrific force in 61. Tacitus, whose sense of drama was attracted by these events, bluntly admits that the immediate cause was the tactlessness, brutality and licentiousness of army officers and treasury officials who partitioned for the Emperor his half share of a great legacy of Prasutagus, allied king of the Iceni. When the queen, omitted from the will, and her two daughters, co-heirs with the Emperor, were maddened by insult and brought arrest, scourging or violation upon themselves, the tribe rose, defeated the legion brought against it and embroiled the Trinovantes in revolt. This was not difficult, for the Trinovantes had been treated as conquered enemies liable to the full severity of Roman rule, and part of their territory had been confiscated to accommodate the new Roman capital and its ex-servicemen settlers. But the outstanding fact is that the revolt hardly spread beyond these limits. The neighbouring areas affected, including the towns of London and St. Albans, were friendly areas. Nor is there evidence of outside help. Even after the defeat of the legion on their frontier, the Brigantes did not stir. The reason for this was that disunity in the royal house of this widely scattered tribe had created a balance of power which curbed the anti-Roman party until, amid the confusion of the Roman Civil War of 69, they drove out the pro-Roman queen Cartimandua. Annexation by Rome then followed as soon as possible.

The annexation of the Brigantes in fact introduced the Romans to a series of problems new to them in Britain. Until then there had been no permanent occupation beyond the lowlands, where control was rendered easy by the simple fact that the lowlanders were principally engaged in cultivating their lands, where Roman officials could find and punish them. But in the Pennines or in Wales it was otherwise. There men lived by flocks and herds rather than by agriculture. Fertile land was restricted to the steep valley sides, since the valley bottoms were still undrained jungle and the hill-tops rocky or peat-covered. Agricultural land was thus rare, and good hill-pastures widely scattered. The Northern and Western peoples thus perforce lived either an agricultural life at poverty level or a pastoral life of seasonal movement. They were less easy to hold down and more prone to strife, brigandage and cattle-raiding. In the lowlands order could be ensured through the local tribal authorities, but the uplands required permanent policing by armed authority. To ensure peace on the borderland of the Roman province a military occupation was an inevitable necessity. This requirement changed the whole character of the British province.

The conquest of the hill-country was not in itself very difficult. The great strongholds, with massive dry-stone defences copied from Southern types, were fewer, though often less accessible. Outstanding examples are Ingleborough, Almondbury and Eston Nab (Yorkshire), Birrenswark (Dumfriesshire), Carrock Fell (Cumberland), Woden Law and the North Eildon

HOD HILL, DORSET
First century A.D. A British fortress, with Roman fort in upper corner

(Roxburghshire), Traprain Law (East Lothian) and Arbory Hill (Lanark-shire). But, however difficult of access, they were the obvious objectives, and many exhibit visible ancient demolition of their defences. Once these outstanding centres were removed, like Tarquin's poppies, the communities they had dominated could offer no further effective resistance from their scattered and defenceless hamlets. And the Roman military machine, half

13

heavy-armed legionaries and half lighter-armed and mobile auxiliary infantry and cavalry, was singularly well adapted for the work of conquest.

The work of settlement was the major difficulty. The first task was to subdivide the tribal districts by a network of garrisons and to dominate the main lines of movement. Central and nodal points were held by auxiliary cavalry, intermediate forts by infantry. All the upland communities of Wales and the Pennines were quickly thus hemmed in and soon the roads, created to link and provision the forts, converted the cordon into a mesh. The network rendered unlawful movement impossible without detection and supervision. The rearward focal points were the legionary fortresses. By A.D. 75 three of them had been fixed at points which they were to occupy for centuries. The Second Legion lay at Caerleon-upon-Usk, keeping an eye upon South Wales with a backward glance across the Bristol Channel. The Twentieth occupied Chester, watching Northern and Central Wales, the Peak and the Western Pennines. The Ninth, later superseded by the Sixth, was stationed at York, surveying the Yorkshire dales and the routes to north and northwest. These great fifty-acre fortresses, with their vast administrative buildings, palatial officers' quarters, granaries, hospitals, barracks and workshops, were an unexampled achievement in planning and organisation. They were the pattern from which, in miniature and simplified form, each of the much smaller five-acre and three-acre forts of the network was copied. When it is appreciated that in Wales and the Pennines there were not less than seventy such forts, a rough but impressive notion is gained of the effort involved in their foundation and maintenance.

The system thus designed was extended by Agricola as far north as the Tay : but there, at the edge of the Highlands, it came to an abrupt stop. For here is another type of mountain land, impenetrable and grim, whose glens offer few through routes and little open country. Even campaigning could not go forward as before, and it was necessary, by combining a flanking movement of troops through Strathmore with forays from the sea, to provoke the Highlanders into pitched battle. The victory gained was decisive but it could not lead to permanent occupation. The step now taken was to block the Highland passes with a series of forts based upon a forward legionary fortress on the Tay.

The furthest northward expansion of the Roman Empire had now been attained. But its strength was almost immediately curtailed by the removal of at least a whole legion from the British garrison. The pressing reason for this reduction was undoubtedly troubles then occurring on the Danube frontier. But no attempt was ever made to replace the troops and it is thus plain that the decision was also based upon other grounds. One reason is obvious. The area comprising Wales, the Pennines and the Scottish Lowlands is larger than the civilian hinterland and its occupation costs must have been very heavy. An attempt to reduce the burden was obviously demanded. But withdrawal meant loss of initiative—safe to sacrifice immediately after a crushing victory, unwise to risk later. Rather more than a generation elapsed before the counter-blow came: at the time of Hadrian's accession, in the summer of 117, but in circumstances upon which neither literature nor archaeology shed light, there was a northern rising, severe enough to call for an expeditionary force from the Continent for a punitive campaign, followed by the replacement of the Ninth Legion by the Sixth. When Britain and other Western provinces received a visit from Hadrian in 122, it was decided to curtail the military area by drawing a frontier barrier right across the sland from Tyne to Solway. This is the great monument known as Hadrian's Wall.

AN AUXILIARY TROOPER IN BATTLE
First century A.D. Tombstone of a Thracian at Cirencester, Gloucestershire

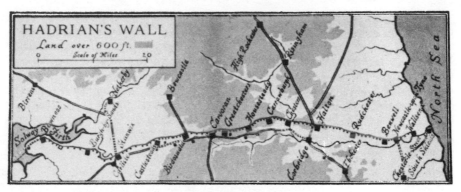

MAP OF HADRIAN'S WALL

THE PACIFICATION

HADRIAN'S new frontier barrier was a continuous wall or rampart, designed in general to block all access from the North, and in particular to prevent infiltration by raiders. It is a far stronger barrier than the corresponding line in Germany, indicating that a massive obstacle was the prime need and that bold attempts to cross it were expected. As first designed, the Wall was to run from Newcastle-upon-Tyne to Bowness-upon-Solway, on a line of great natural strength : it was equipped with turrets and milecastles, or fortlets a mile apart, for patrols; and the fighting garrison was to lie behind it. While the work was in progress the plan was modified. The fighting garrison was moved into new forts on the Wall itself, the forts were increased in number, the Wall was extended down the Tyne to Wallsend and the rear of the now compact zone was sealed off by a boundary dyke, commonly called the Vallum. These changes were all directed towards increased control ; indeed, Hadrian's Wall marks the apogee of control by cordon. In particular, moving the fighting garrison on to the Wall facilitated speedy interception in the controlled field of manœuvre in front of the line. The result was a barrier of immense strength, endowed with a highly flexible defence, designed to roll up the enemy against the obstacle which he was attempting to cross.

The weakness of the Wall lies in the fact that its line, a first-class choice from the purely military point of view, was not in contact with the centres of disaffection beyond it, whence raids could still be organised and large-scale attacks planned with impunity. On the other hand, the fact that archaeology informs us of no destruction on Hadrian's Wall during its first years justifies the assumption that the Wall was a success. This explains why it must undoubtedly have been tempting to get rid of the political difficulty by including the centres of unrest in Southern Scotland behind a

AN AUXILIARY TROOPER'S BRONZE PARADE-MASK
First century A.D. From Newstead, Roxburghshire

AN OFFICIAL BRONZE CORN-MEASURE

A.D. 90-92.   From Carvoran, Northumberland

GILDED BRONZE STATUE OF HERCULES

Second-third century A.D. From Birdoswald, Hadrian's Wall

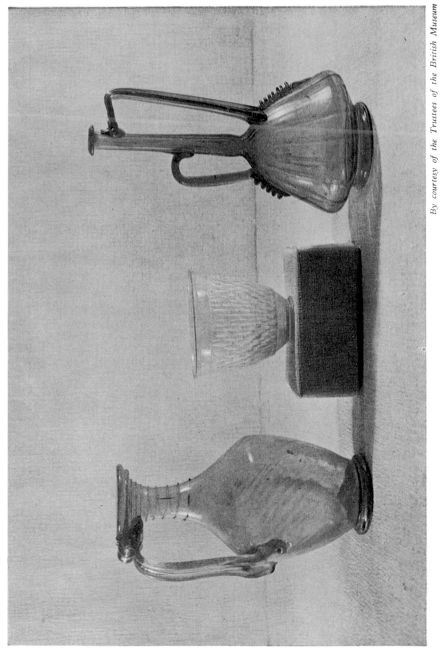

ROMAN GLASS TABLE-WARE

Third century A.D. Imported to Britain from the Rhineland

new Wall between Forth and Clyde; while, from the point of view of the Empire at large, the conquered tribes on unconditional surrender could be made to supply so large a quota of recruits for the Roman auxiliary army on the Continent that expansion could be made to yield a valuable asset in man-power. Thus, odd though it may seem to jettison Hadrian's Wall so soon, there were good reasons to dictate the change. The new advance was undertaken in A.D. 139-142, by Lollius Urbicus, and Hadrian's Wall as such was abandoned. The doors were taken off the milecastle gateways and the rearward boundary dyke was systematically breached.

The new Wall, on the Forth-Clyde isthmus, was only half as long as Hadrian's Wall and its design was different. The Wall was of turf, a good enough obstacle, but cheaper and easier to build, and its ditch was larger. There were neither milecastles nor turrets, but nineteen forts sufficiently close together to view all forward terrain and to concentrate a bigger intercepting force with great speed. The impression conveyed is that the designers expected larger raiding parties and were determined to intercept them with overwhelming force before they crossed the barrier. The main line of approach, on the East, was held well in advance of the Wall, so as to prevent the occupation of Fife as a raiders' base. How other forward areas were treated is unknown. The hinterland, from Forth to Tyne, was supplied with the usual strategic network of roads, garrisoned by widely separated large forts, many holding cavalry, and by block-house posts connected with a long-range signalling system.

The new distribution of power thus shifted the military centre of gravity to the Lowlands of Scotland. This was achieved only at the risk of thinning out the garrisons of the occupied area behind them. Thinning had proved safe in Wales, where the tribes had in the past been so harried as to have learnt their lesson : it was untried among the Brigantes, where, in contrast with Wales, many sections of the tribe had been absorbed into the province relatively unscathed. An adverse result soon came. The slackening of tension induced a great rising in 155-158, in which the breaking of fixed tribal boundaries may have been the outstanding cause of trouble. In 184 there was another kind of danger. The northern Wall was overwhelmed in a large invasion, attended by heavy casualties on the Roman side. Finally, in 197, came the heaviest disaster of all. At this time the Imperial succession had broken down and Army marshals were disputing their rival claims to the principate. In this contest the governor of Britain, Clodius Albinus, took a leading part and fought out his claim upon the Continent with the aid of almost the whole army of Britain. When he lost and most of his army was annihilated, the Northern tribes broke in, swept southwards as far as York and Chester and laid waste the forts and countryside everywhere. Archaeology tells us that the hated fortifications were so vindictively thrown down that they had often for long stretches to be rebuilt from the very foundations. To secure conditions for a fresh start the new legate of Severus

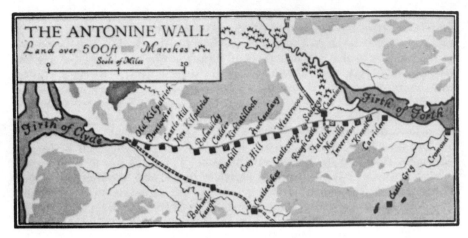

MAP OF THE ANTONINE WALL

bought the tribes off, and in ten years reconstruction had passed beyond Hadrian's Wall.

Now came the time for a punitive expedition, occasioned by sharp reaction of the Northern tribes to the new vigour of the provincial government. After a year's preparation on the spot Severus and his elder son took the field, leaving the younger son behind as Emperor-administrator ; and, disregarding appeals for terms, in two seasons' campaigning reached deep into northern Scotland without achieving a pitched battle. Peace was arranged, only to be broken by the barbarians with maddening inconstancy, and the old Emperor, like another and later Hammer of the Scots, decided that annihilation was the only solution left. Fate favoured Caledonia, for Severus died amid preparations for the new campaign.

For three years Britain had absorbed the personal attention of Emperors, but the moment of a new accession was no time for this to continue. After arranging terms with the Northerners, Antoninus and Geta, with the redoubtable Empress-Dowager, returned to Rome. Garrisons were evacuated and Hadrian's Wall was once again the frontier barrier. But now the system of interception differed. A wide strip extending to the Cheviots, the natural boundary between England and Scotland, was held in great force by outpost-forts on which were based strong frontier patrols. Consonantly, many forts on Hadrian's Wall received enlarged garrisons, while the milecastles and turrets of the Wall-patrols became less important. The meaning of these measures is clear. The Wall remained no less emphatically than before a barrier against infiltration, but concentrated attacks were to be met far beyond it. Public life beyond the new frontier was strictly controlled. Arrangements in Central Europe suggest that assemblages would be allowed only at stated times and places under Roman supervision : and another highly significant fact is that fortifications of Lowland hill-towns dated to this time resemble those of villages. But commerce flourished: minor manufactured goods from the Roman province abound in the Lowlands, which were becoming what would nowadays be called a sphere of influence attached to Rome by treaty. Amicability would be increased by another factor also. From the time of Severus onwards, while military units retained their ancient names, the basis of recruitment became steadily more local and a generation later soldiers with serving sons might obtain land upon lease in their garrison area. These developments represent a social change of major importance, amounting to the creation of a territorial army, increasingly native to its province. The effect upon frontier relations was unquestionably profound. It is now that the village settlements outside the frontier forts of Hadrian's Wall grew to large size, covering a bigger area than the tightly packed forts themselves.

Who, then, were now the enemies ? Under Severus, the principal enemies had still been the Northern tribes, the Maeatae, whose name is associated with the head of the Firth of Forth and Strathearn, and the Caledonii, centred in the Highlands. A century later, the emphasis has shifted. The Northern folk beyond the Tay have become known generically as Picti, by which the Roman meant the tattooed folk. Their attacks are coupled with those of the Saxons and Irish, and literary sources make it very evident that most of them were sea-raids with light pirate craft. The new need was to protect all the coastlands of Britain from pillage and kidnapping. But it must not be assumed that the problem became urgent everywhere at once. The first task seems to have been the protection of the South-East, the wealthiest part of the province and the easiest of landfalls from the Continent. By the close of the third century coastal forts of the newest type, with high walls and enfilading towers, were being erected in Kent, and the system spread until it reached from Wash to Solent, a tract officially known as the Saxon Shore. Measures in the Bristol Channel are represented by a fort in the new style at Cardiff. All these forts were intimately linked with naval defence, their sites being suited for sea-patrols as well as land forces. Indeed, the fleet for Britain, no longer tied to cross-Channel headquarters at Boulogne, must have been completely reorganised to meet the new situation. Camouflaged scout-ships, for example, were invented to meet the Picts, just as Rome had copied pirate craft in the Adriatic centuries before. To meet landings in force, mobile units of mailed cavalry were developed under a Count of the Saxon Shore and a Duke of the Britains (the four British provinces organised after 297). The general success of the system must be inferred from the fact that it drove the enemy to combine, an event almost without precedent in the barbarian world. In A.D. 368 the Picts, Irish, Saxons and Franks set upon the province jointly in force, killing the Count and ambushing the Duke. The effect upon the country districts was severe and led to a still further extension of the coastal defences. The Yorkshire coast was now fortified with massive watch-towers, linked with central interceptor garrisons, which seem to have ensured renewed prosperity. It was plain that the Wall was becoming an anachronism. The outpost forts had been gradually given up, some before 367 and the rest at that date, while the rulers of the tribes beyond, notably the Damnonii of Clydesdale and the Votadini of Lothian, had become allies of Rome, fully responsible for the defence of their own territory. In 394, when Stilicho had to reorganise the northern defences after the usurper Magnus Maximus had evacuated the Wall and lost the bulk of British garrison troops in his bid for Empire, the Wall was not restored. Garrisons still held important points immediately to the south, but many of these were stripped for the defence of the Empire in Europe against Alaric. In this devolution the province was but following the pattern of the times.

A ROMAN FORT IN THE PENNINES
Whitley Castle, Northumberland

TRIBAL COMMUNITIES AND THE CITY-STATE

ROMAN belief in the urban community was based upon traditional experience. In Mediterranean lands the relatively small and jealously guarded cultivable areas had to be controlled from a single fortified centre, and this was the basis of the Roman conception of the political unit as essentially urban. In Britain, as in other provinces of the Roman West, the problem was to apply this conception to tribal communities. The point of contact was the fact that most Celtic tribes had long possessed a central-ised government, through nobles in council headed by a king or by elected magistrates, which could be adapted and used for Roman local adminis-tration. But the nearest approach to a town was the great central fortress or *oppidum*, where everything centred about the noble households or the tribal host. The most advanced British tribal aristocrat would have recoiled from exchanging his local freedom of action, whether in fortress or estate, for residence in a central community of Roman pattern. Thus, from the first, the acceptance of Roman civilisation was for the British tribal notable a compromise. Town-life was accepted as something periodic and im-permanent, part of a dual existence in which residence in town was required for the periodic conduct of government, while country life was demanded by the almost continuous claims made by the management and enjoyment of a great estate. Which part of the duality came uppermost would depend upon individual inclination and wealth. But wealth was so universally de-rived from landed estate that country residence for owners was the basic requirement. Far from diminishing this need, Roman rule increased it: for it was the tribal councillors who became guarantors for payment of taxation, whether in kind or in money, if production or communal resources failed. It was a sense of putting first things first, quite apart from ancestral habit, which based the Romano-British aristocracy upon the country rather than town.

Unwillingness to shed ancestral habits, however, was undoubtedly the basis of a recorded initial reluctance to adopt Roman dress or the Latin language. But it was not long before Roman ways became paramount, owing to the attraction of Roman material civilisation. Roman building afforded an elegance and comfort which were the true concomitants of the luxury articles long imported and enjoyed by British nobles. Above all, the Em-peror's peace ensured ease in social intercourse and interchange of ideas and time for their enjoyment. Freedom from fear, accompanied by wealth, opened new fields of emulation and ambition.

At this point the Roman government had plans ready. First, standards had to be created, whether their attainment was painful or not. Seven years after the conquest there was established at Camulodunum a new Roman capital, peopled with veteran legionaries and equipped with public buildings intended to display the new elegance of life and to be a model of Roman ways. Foremost among the new structures was the Temple of Claudius, centre for provincial worship of the Emperor and focus of provincial loyalty to Rome. The cult and ritual were maintained by a priesthood filled annually by a provincial notable and his wife, chosen from among the different tribes in council. This was a costly honour, involving the expense of public festivals and contests, athletic, literary and musical. In Gaul, the parallel institution, which replaced a native annual tribal congress, was a great social and political success. But in Germany, where there existed no such traditional foundation, it almost failed ; while in Britain little is heard of it, though it must be underlined that the silence may be due to scant survival of Roman inscriptions rather than real failure : for when the Temple went up in flames in the rebellion of 61, it was restored from its ashes and the project was not abandoned. Nor was the rebuilt *colonia*, as these chartered towns of Roman citizens were called, a failure. It was large (108 acres), by contemporary standards for such foundations; and discoveries show that it was wealthy and prosperous, a good pattern of what Romanisation meant. Further, there soon followed, towards the end of the first century, two other foundations of the same kind, each covering about 40 acres, at Gloucester for the South-West and at Lincoln for the North. Remains from both these *coloniae* indicate the same comfortable prosperity. Indeed, at Lincoln the prosperity may well be called superabundant: for the town doubled its size, so that the notable remains of its first wall and gates upon the hilltop embrace less than half the ultimate walled area, extending down to the riverbank. The noble colonnade in the Bailgate and some striking remains of sculpture in stone and bronze attest its urbanity.

The incentive to Romanisation provided by alluring patterns was thus supplied. The second stage in the governmental plan was to promote its imitation. At least one tribal capital, that of the faithful King-Legate Cogidumnus at Chichester, had already begun to equip itself by his royal and legatine authority with public buildings of Roman style and function. Presently the provincial governors, with Imperial approval, began to encourage the foundation of tribal capitals in territories where initiative had not been taken. Literature assigns the start of this movement to the Flavian age, though its culmination was almost fifty years later.

The town-plans of smaller tribal capitals reveal in general terms what was meant. The town site, whether previously inhabited or not, was provided with a new and complete system of regular streets of chess-board plan, centred about a majestic local government building, which combined the functions of market-place, town-hall and law-court. At the same time other public buildings, paid for out of tribal revenue or given by tribal notables, were projected on the same scale. These would comprise such edifices as public baths and temples, or an amphitheatre, theatre, market-hall, commemorative arch and so forth, the selection being dependent upon the wealth of the community or the desires of individual donors. To present

CAST OF THE DEDICATION-TABLET OF THE FORUM, WROXETER, A.D. 129-130

IMP. CAES. DIVI TRAIANI PARTHI / CI FIL. DIVI NERVAE NEPOTI TRA / IANO HADRIANO AVG. PONTIFI / CI MAXIMO TRIB. POT. XIIII COS. III P.P. / CIVITAS CORNOVIORVM

such buildings to the community was the new way of winning family fame or local prestige. Individuality, however, is most obvious in private buildings. These occupy the chess-board plan in such a fashion as to indicate that plots of land could be bought unhampered by close regulations as to style or plan of the building erected thereon. The shops, long buildings with narrow street-frontage and an upper storey containing stores or the shopkeeper's dwelling, jostle one another along the main thoroughfare. The houses, large and small, sprawl about in their own grounds. The contrast with true town-houses, filling the entire street frontage and abutting upon neighbouring buildings with urbanity, is as sharp as it could possibly be. As to society, the houses represent at least two grades; the compact dwelling of the small administrative official is readily distinguished from the spacious houses of the tribal councillors. All have much space for gardens, and this love of flowery surroundings is not confined to domestic buildings. The temples, nearly always of non-Roman plan, frequently lie in big enclosures obviously devoted to flowers and trees.

Romano-British towns, though planned upon the same general principles, were not uniform creations. All exhibit an almost deceptive regularity of street-plan, but the arrangement in each is so different that all possess a marked individuality. This refreshing lack of uniformity, allied to respect for standards, is due to the prudent policy of the Roman government; for, while town-life was officially encouraged, communities were not as a rule permitted to embark upon heavy expenditure without ascertaining that they were able to bear it. Even private endowments and benefactions received no sanction without examination of incidental public outlay. The aspect of a town very fairly mirrored the resources of the community concerned.

Four towns whose planning is known in some detail amply reflect these conditions. At St. Albans, the ancient *Verulamium*, chief town of the Catuvellauni, an early start had been made in Romanisation. According to Tacitus, it was a considerable place when it perished in the Boudiccan

23

revolt of 61, but the town as first rebuilt was of modest size. Two generations later a much larger town was springing to life. It boasted a noble *forum*, architecturally the most ambitious in Britain, a theatre of semi-Roman type, a market-hall, some fine temples, two triumphal arches and massive defences entered through imposing town-gates. The chess-board plan is relieved from monotony by the fact that Watling Street of earlier Roman days breaks across it and pulls the public buildings out of centre. Obviously this single trunk road attracted all the showy buildings of the town. In Silchester, *Calleva Atrebatum*, it was otherwise. As first planned, this town was one of the large tribal capitals of the island, with a wide-meshed chess-board street-plan covering an irregular octagonal area of 230 acres bounded by earthwork defences. Shops line the main street: there is a large central local government building. But other public buildings are so scattered as to tell of haphazard creation based upon private donations of land and buildings. The town had been left to spread radially along the four main roads that met there. The private houses are notable. Some twenty-five are large straggling dwellings, country houses transferred to town. They can be recognised as the dwellings of the tribal notables. The smaller houses, hardly more numerous, count as those of administrative officers or merchants.

At Caerwent, *Venta Silurum*, conditions are again different, to judge from the excavated half of the area. This South Welsh town is small, only 45 acres in extent. The main street is crowded with shops, and its centre is occupied by a local government building. But very few houses are large or sumptuous, and most are small and simply appointed. This implies a tribal aristocracy concentrated upon its country estates and unwilling in the main to build town-houses. The town is left to permanent administrative staff and to merchants. It may be that this remote canton was too poor to rise to higher civilisation : but it can be no coincidence that among the Silures resistance to Rome had burnt fierce and long. The same phenomenon, of the small town, is seen in the fourth example, Caister by Norwich, the ancient *Venta Icenorum*. This was the capital of a tribe whose wild revolt, the product of bitter disillusionment, had been followed by savage repression. In lands where Romanisation was sown in blood the new town-life was plainly a more stunted growth : it was an outstanding achievement to make it flower at all.

The technical executants of this urbanisation were no doubt Roman contractors from the civil areas of southern Europe. To them can be traced the Italian marble veneers for public buildings or the stiffly correct architectural details from the local government buildings of Silchester and elsewhere. But these and other edifices also bear the mark of another influence. In the Roman world at large there was no obvious distinction between architect and civil or military engineer, and military engineers were freely drafted on service to official civilian work and frequently went into such

CARVED STONE CAPITAL
From Cirencester, *Corinium Dobunnorum*

work on retirement. In heavily garrisoned provinces the military architects
already had much to do, and it is not surprising to find plentiful reflection
of their work in British towns. The local government buildings of the tribal
capitals, mostly halls of justice or exchange combined with a market-place
surrounded by shops and offices, copy the headquarters buildings of the
legionary fortress so closely that the origin of their design is not to be
doubted. No less evident is the kinship between the Silchester public baths
and a military bath-house. The military land engineer is also evident in
bridges and urban water-supplies. No example is known in Britain of a
monumental road-bridge arched in stone, as opposed to the military type
with stone piers and wooden superstructure. No Romano-British town has
yet furnished an example of the stately civilian aqueduct. All conduits so
far traced, as at Wroxeter, Silchester, Caister by Norwich, Dorchester, or
Lincoln, are the underground gravitational pipe-lines which were the
common military type. Here, as in the street-planning, the military hand
is revealed.

This is not to say that all architecture was of military inspiration or
that military architects never got away from military design. Even the
buildings described offered the widest scope for variation. The market-place
at Verulamium is purely civilian in design, reminiscent of such squares in
Roman Africa. The great thermal establishment at the curative hot springs

of Bath is equally civilian in feeling and inspiration. The Leicester baths are attached to a great pillared hall which, like its smaller counterpart at Caerwent, may owe something to the legionary *schola*, or recreation room. But the general impression is anything but military.

The social effect of this fostered urbanisation plainly also differed much in different districts. In the West, Wroxeter (*Viroconium Cornoviorum*), which had blossomed under Hadrian into a town almost as large as Verulamium, was devastated at the close of the third century and recovered only in part; but little Caerwent (*Venta Silurum*) remained an active centre until well into the Dark Ages. In the South, Silchester was reduced in the second century from 230 acres to 100 acres and lasted tolerably prosperous and active into the fifth century in this smaller rationalised form. At Verulamium, on the other hand, second-century prosperity was succeeded by great decay of larger house-property in the third century, followed in turn by a vigorous but brief recovery in the fourth century and the ultimate abandonment of much of the residential area for a restricted but intensive concentration round the market and administrative buildings. In the North, at Aldborough (*Isurium Brigantum*), the fourth century was a time of wealth and prosperity, when domestic buildings were actively embellished. Positive generalisation upon such diverse evidence might be misleading, but negative points emerge. The tribal capitals as a whole neither grew nor attracted wealthy residents. They remained administrative and market towns. Nor do they seem to have attracted much industry. But here we must pause, remembering that many of these cantonal capitals like Chichester, Winchester, Cirencester or Leicester are so densely overlaid by modern buildings that they cannot contribute to the picture. It nevertheless remains true that Roman Britain was primarily a rural province, whose principal citizens led a life of isolation for which they were ultimately to pay in blood and tears. The attempt to orientate the tribal outlook towards urban life came to grief upon the rock of individuality.

A KEEPSAKE FROM HADRIAN'S WALL FOUND IN WILTSHIRE
Second-third century A.D. Bronze enamelled cup
engraved with the names of Wall-forts

A BOY IN A CHARIOT-RACE
Probably third century A.D.
Fragment of a relief in stone from Lincoln

THE IMPACT OF THE NEW CULTURE

ROMAN culture was in many respects so new to the Britons that the
first close contact must have been wholly bewildering. The army,
which spread over their land and was organised for permanent service
upon a scale which no barbarian had ever conceived, must have come as a
shattering revelation of the material power of Rome. Hard upon its arrival
followed the road-building, to which British labour-gangs contributed sweat
and toil ; and this was something more startling than the railway development of centuries later. When it is realised that in an Imperial province
all this and other benefits or burdens were at the Emperor's behest, it is
easy to see how every Briton would quickly appreciate the reality of the
Emperor as a power which it would not seem unnatural to reverence as

27

divine. Disbelief, coarse and cynical, or disclaimers, sagacious and forthright, originated rather from the Roman side.

Emperor-worship was chosen as the core and symbol of the new civilisation, and was served by an imported religion, wherein the central feature of the calendar was the gathering in council of tribal representatives at a festival in honour of the Emperor. This implied a routine of elaborate ritual and sacrifices, punctuated by feast days and contests in a new language and idiom. The idiom in particular must have been arresting and challenging. British art had owed its beauty to sensitive manipulation of a limited stock-in-trade of conventional flowing curves. It had deliberately turned its back upon accurate or literal portrayal, its animals being phantasies, its human forms—whether earthly or divine—monstrous and magical, remote from actual experience. But the central figure in the new Roman world of representation was the Emperor, a living image frozen into stone or metal and idealised by the very act. As a type of ideal humanity, whether on the coinage or in statuary, the Emperor symbolised the Roman world and its standards.

But in all provinces and certainly in Britain, this aristocratic ceremonial of official creation was aloof from the general public who sought and received their expression of loyalty at other levels. It was a matter of course that the Roman chartered towns or *coloniae*, as at York and Lincoln, had corporate priesthoods of the mercantile class charged with Emperor-worship. But nothing is known of its celebration in the tribal capitals. To judge from the inscriptions of a principal magistrate in the East Yorkshire tribal centre of *Petuaria* (Brough-on-Humber) or of the Shropshire tribe of the Cornovii, loyalty took the form of direct honorific dedication of buildings either to the living Emperor or to the "active power" (*numen*) of the Emperors living and deceased. This dedication to the *numen Augusti* or the *numina Augustorum* is particularly common in the Roman military world, where it is frequently associated with the worship of another undoubted god. It was a conception which reached all ranks of society, from peasantry conscripted for their twenty-five years of service with the auxiliaries, to Roman-citizen legionaries and the officers of all units. It finds its place not only among serving soldiers but among veterans and heads of village communities and occurs, however rarely, in private country-houses. Of its pervasiveness and reality there can be no doubt.

Education is a phase of Romano-British life of which we hear little. But there is no doubt that the Latin language and Graeco-Roman modes of thought were the standard. Latin was the vehicle of all official business and of commerce : it was also the channel through which Greek thought was accessible. It is clear that to the average Briton of education Latin was sufficient, and that to many the Latin learnt in speech and writing would be barrack-room Latin, a *sermo castrensis* of a colloquial, racy and eminently practical kind. In estimating educative influences, it is of importance to

BRONZE HEAD OF THE EMPEROR CLAUDIUS
A.D. 50-61. Loot from Colchester found in the river Alde, Suffolk

recall that Britons drafted into military service automatically picked up Latin as their everyday language of drill, orders and routine : just as for the army in Britain, drawn from all quarters of the Empire, it was the only medium of spoken contact with their environment and the only language that men would learn to write. Not that native languages necessarily died, but they were useless for official and general cosmopolitan intercourse. Echoes of everyday Latin come down in imprecations hung up in shrines or consigned to sacred wells, or in workmen's scrawls : and a considerably higher stage is represented by business-contracts from London dealing with everyday local transactions and couched in terse and inelegant commercial language.

The higher stages are more difficult to apprehend. Tacitus indicates that about A.D. 81 the governor Agricola was forwarding the education of British aristocratic youths. It seems to have been this programme which had brought Demetrius of Tarsus, a Greek grammarian, or teacher of senior boys, to Britain before 84. Juvenal, writing about 128, mentions not only British lawyers taught by Gauls but contracts for teachers of rhetoric, the university stage of ancient education; as if the British communities had by then taken enlightened action in the matter of teaching their upper-class youth. In the later third century the British father of the usurper-Emperor Bonosus is recorded to have been a rhetorician, and his marriage to a Gaulish lady may suggest where he got his training overseas. Archaeology has a little to contribute. A large country-house at Otway, Kent, has yielded a fragment of wall-painting depicting Vergilian scenes, headed with quotations from this first of Roman poets. A great pavement at Low Ham, Somerset, portrays Dido and Aeneas. This must represent families fond of classic literature, just as the Aldborough mosaic pavement with a personification of Mount Helicon, labelled in Greek, denotes regard for the Muses. The ultimate effect at least is plain. When, under Christianity, religion became subject to definition and regulation, Britain's contribution both to orthodoxy and heresy is praised or condemned with such emphasis as to imply forcible power of advocacy. Little survives of these writings. St. Patrick, always protesting his meagre erudition, writes a crisp and forthright style. A debased form of the erudite style is exemplified five generations later by Gildas the Wise, who writes in a strangely provincial mixture of Latin and Greek and Hebrew and local words. The tortured ingenuity offends; but what impresses is the extensive vocabulary, still packed with literary allusion, and the complex grammatical construction. As a survival of a culture, long isolated and driven in upon itself, it is no bad testimony to the power and accomplishment of Roman education in these islands.

To separate education from religion in the classical world was impossible and unthinkable. The religious story, in lively and human form, was so much the vehicle of standards of morality and conduct, or of legends of passion and prowess, that it coloured every branch of Roman literature

BRONZE HEAD OF SUL-MINERVA
Second century A.D.   Found at Bath, *Aquae Sulis*, in 1727

and art. In addition, the intimate mixture of Greek and Roman civilisation
produced a habit of religious exchange and interchange, in which the gods
of Italy and Greece came to form a common heritage acceptable to either
race : while their joint contact with the Middle East introduced new and
broader equations. In the Roman pantheon, while Olympians took pre-
cedence, and the tutelary gods of Rome had their paramount sphere, ample
room was left for other local deities, who might or might not be recognised
as powerful enough to deserve equation with a Greek or Roman god. In
the Celtic world, however, to which Britain belonged, the conception of

31

godhead, further from man and closer to nature, was less concrete. Gods could exchange functions with bewildering frequency. They could be at once plural and singular and were by no means always human in form. Often, indeed, they remained immanent and formless, and, while this type of deity existed in the Graeco-Roman world as a survival from ancient belief, the tendency to portray deities with human form and attributes had there long ousted the primitive conception. Thus, when the Roman was confronted by Celtic gods, his first act was to define them in terms of his own pantheon, and exchange upon this basis ended in a victory for Rome: for the Briton, faced with the problem of bringing his deities as well as himself into line with the new world of which he formed part, chose the Roman mode of presentation as the vehicle of his revised and enlarged ideas, just as he unhesitatingly chose Latin as the medium of dedication. The change was sharper and more complete than in Gaul, where old-established cults did not at once abandon the Gaulish language or artistic idiom, though it is always possible that in this regard Britain has surprises in store. But few British deities are unendowed with a Graeco-Roman synonym or represented in anything but classical garb. On the other hand, the number of British gods or goddesses that survive on these terms is eloquent both of Roman tolerance and British tenacity. Apollo-Maponus, Victoria-Brigantia, Mars-Cocidius, or Silvanus-Cocidius, and Mars-Belatucadrus in the North, Sul-Minerva, Mars-Teutates or Nodens-Silvanus in the South, and the ubiquitous Matres, or Mother-goddesses, form a goodly group of native conceptions presented in the humane conventions of classical art.

The new conventions adopted for religious art thus played no unimportant part in the new culture. But the content as well as the form of Roman religion also had its part to play. The religion of the Roman State and army, dim or impersonal to-day, was a living reality to those who carried out its ritual for the safety and welfare of those institutions. Its performance was therefore obligatory, whatever personal devotions—they were many and various—an individual might privately indulge. Jupiter, Best and Greatest, protector of the Roman State, received the major share of worship and dedications, but many other religious feasts, officially calendared for the army and connected with the very foundation-legends and growth of Rome, were kept with due solemnity or gaiety. Soldiers in the legions were Roman citizens already ; soldiers in the auxiliaries became Roman citizens upon honourable discharge. All had therefore an interest, actual or prospective, in the welfare of the Roman body-politic. The meaning of the feasts and the beliefs connected with them must thus have been learnt by all and in such lessons graphic representation took an important part. For example, Hercules was elaborated into a type of the divine or spiritual labourer for mankind and so into a personification of the labours of the Emperor or his agents. The birthday of Rome, again, afforded an occasion for addresses upon Rome's ancient grandeur and enduring glory. Thus, Rome's past and

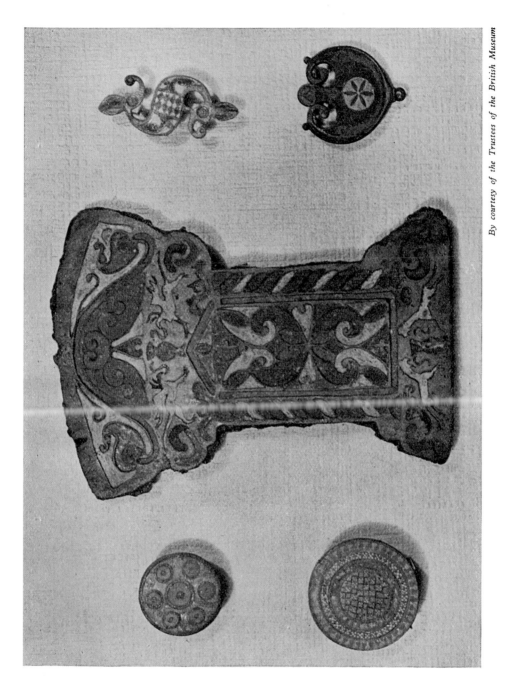

ROMAN ENAMELLED ALTAR PLAQUE FROM THE THAMES, AND GROUP OF ENAMELLED BROOCHES

Second-third century A.D.

MOSAIC PAVEMENT FROM LITTLECOTE PARK, RAMSBURY, WILTSHIRE

Second-third century A.D.   Engraving by George Vertue, 1730

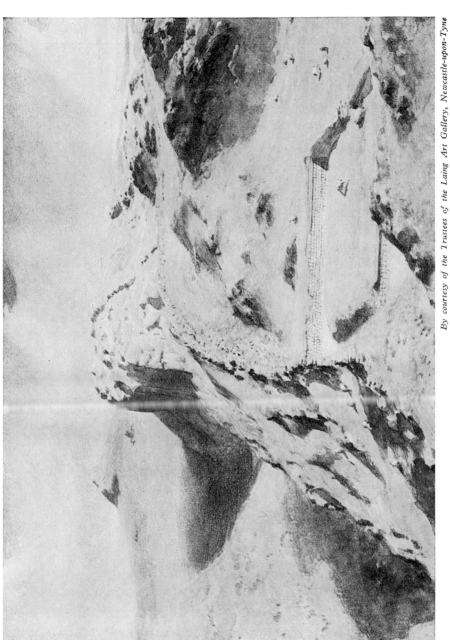

HADRIAN'S WALL, AND CASTLE NICK MILECASTLE

A.D. 122-126.   Near Crag Lough Northumberland.   Water colour by H. B. Richardson, 1848

ROMAN WEST GATE, LINCOLN, IN 1836
Late first century A.D.   Lithograph by Samuel Tuke

achievements were regarded as part of the heritage of all who fought for her. And when the native soldier retired, these things were by him imparted to his children or friends or village community. There was thus a double educative movement, from upper and from lower ranks of society, which met in the general public.

For that general public, the impact of Roman culture was nowhere more evident than in material civilisation. The Roman age was an age of workshop manufacture of goods in large quantity, serving an immense expanding market rendered easy of access by transport facilities of an entirely new kind. New materials and new tools and methods produced a revolution in almost every walk of life. Iron tools of every sort in quantity, new building materials of brick and tile, cut stone and cement, resulted in improved methods of carpentry and masons' work. Furniture of Roman taste and manner abounded. For the table, all kinds of wares were available, from bronze and earthenware cooking-pans and dishes to abundant plain wares, produced in improved kilns and imitating Roman metallic models, or to the universal bright and attractive vermilion Samian ware, whose forms, either plain or decorated with vigorous moulded patterns and scenes, were themselves distant echoes of the chased and moulded silver ware which decked the wealthiest sideboards. Glass-ware, of graceful outline and delicate tint or deep translucent colouring, added further beauty to the table. But the most enduring furnishings were the mosaic pavements, seldom now polished and lustrous, but still exciting wonder by their bold patterns and vigorous figure-work. Enough remains to afford a fleeting glimpse of the painted wall-plaster which normally went with them : but it is too often forgotten that the mosaics themselves echo no less elaborate carpets and tapestries which are mentioned in literature and survive in fragments in the sands of Egypt.

Although much of this material was so novel and so intimately connected with imported standards of life, detailed study of the later developments in many fields shows interesting native variants. For the new technique and styles were readily applicable to native architectural types. The native temple, a tall round or square building, with surrounding veranda or colonnade, was before Roman times a structure of painted timber, frequently adorned with putrefying heads of slain warriors. This gave way to a building of the same plan in mortared stone or tile, decorated with classical conventions. There was also at least one house-type which seems confined to Celtic lands and is clearly derived from a long pillared hall in timber framing. In pottery manufacture the native potter adapted himself to Roman fashions, though isolated districts retained old styles, while in others forms might change when composition and finish did not. Even in decoration the free style of applied decoration of the Castor potteries retains much of the Celtic facility in rhythmic curves, and a thorough study of local wares will reveal many minor differences. In small decorative metal-work the native craftsman held his own. The brooches of Roman Britain owe

33

TABLE LAMP-STAND IN BRONZE
Second century A.D.   Found at Flixborough, Lincolnshire

much to Continental inspiration in the earlier phase. But two widespread
types conspicuously manifest the old British genius in manipulating and
transforming classical design. The first is the so-called dragonesque brooch,
in which the old interlocking trumpet-pattern grows into a gay and animated

34

writing mass of curves, like a sea-horse or a
dragon. The second is the adaptation of the
acanthus motif to the native trumpet-brooch
with vitality and richness. Much rarer is the
application of pure Celtic decoration to a Roman
type of brooch, as in the famous Aesica brooch
from Hadrian's Wall; and it is significant that
this example belongs to the northern fringe of
the province, just as the bull-headed trumpet-
brooches from Wroxeter and Caernarvon belong
to its western bounds. When these were extin-
guished nothing so notable took their place, but
an important native art which survived was enamelling. True enamelling remained to decorate
brooches and buttons and harness equipment, but
was enriched by new and vivid colours as its pri-
mary purpose, to imitate coral, was forgotten. It
was, however, applied in a new fashion to objects
of Roman form, decorated with Roman patterns.
The Bartlow Hills ritual vase, the Braughing and
Longfaugh ladles or the London altar-piece, are
sumptuous examples of the application of the ancient art to objects and ornament of the new culture. Another development was the cutting of thin
cross-sections of fused bundles of multi-coloured
glass rods, arranged to form minute but vivid patterns, for application to roundels or plate brooches
with striking polychrome effect, in rich contrast
to the gleaming bronze or silver frame. This taste
for polychromy is a Celtic phenomenon. During
the Roman expansion Greek travellers had ob-
served the variegated tunics and striped tartan
cloaks of the Gauls. And while evidence of this
taste survives in small objects, it must not be
forgotten that it also affected large ones.

There is good reason to think that nearly all
Romano-British sculpture was painted, in a riot
of colour which transformed the carving into
a background for paint, redeeming its often
pedestrian quality and picking out otherwise
unheeded detail. Here native and Roman conventions met and produced something rich and
strange, as virile as medieval art and as much
the product of a fusion of culture.

CHAIR-LEG CARVED FROM
KIMMERIDGE SHALE
Probably third century A.D.
Found at Dorchester, 1937

35

PLOUGHMAN AND OXEN
Probably third century A.D.
Bronze group from Piercebridge, Co. Durham

ECONOMIC DEVELOPMENTS

OUR knowledge of economics in Roman Britain depends very largely upon archaeology. Even ancient descriptions of the road-system, which was as vital to the island as railways now are, are not written from the trader's standpoint. They are official itineraries, or documents derived from them, intended for use with the Imperial posting-service, which was an intricate system of conveyances, post-houses and rest-houses maintained exclusively for the use of government travellers. The road-system is in fact considerably more extensive than these documents would suggest, though they include many main routes. It was laid out primarily for military needs, but from the first it was desirable to connect the main allied tribal centres with the provincial fiscal administration and with the military areas which they were to supply. For example, the famous Fosse Way, transformed from an ancient native traffic-route to the lateral communication behind the Claudian Humber-Severn frontier, also links the three tribal centres of the Dumnonii, Dobunni and Coritani; and the roads from terminal and intermediate points on the Fosse Way to the two centres of Colchester (*Camulodunum*) and London (*Londinium*), though intended by their official creators to link the periphery with the centre and with the Channel ports, are also so contrived as to include the bulk of the tribal capitals. The exception is Stane Street, the London-Chichester road, serving the capital of the King-Legate Cogidumnus. But the network soon extended to minor centres and this may well be regarded as a fiscal measure, designed sometimes to develop productive regions, but more often to facilitate collection of taxes in kind and local administration.

Beyond the Fosse Way there were from the first important roads to the legionary fortresses of *Glevum* (Gloucester) and *Viroconium* (Wroxeter) and to the south shore of the Humber. When the advance into the mountain lands took place, it was followed by a vast extension of the road-system with an entirely new purpose. It was an elementary requirement in the military zone that all forts had to be linked with their bases and supporting-stations, to facilitate the movement of regular supplies and of reinforcements. But there was also the policing of the conquered territory to plan, wherein the roads served as lines for cordons to intercept unlawful movement of stock or people. The military areas of Wales, the Pennines and Southern Scotland were thus furnished with a much closer network of roads than the civilian areas behind them.

If, however, the road-system was thus primarily designed for official purposes, it was at the same time not ill-adapted to carry trade. It connected all the principal major and minor civil centres, and notably the markets of those tribal capitals whose urbanisation it was desired to foster. The roads carried much private traffic. In particular, we can trace the movement of heavy commodities. Wine and oil, in casks or heavy corded jars, went everywhere. Building materials were widely distributed. Foreign marbles came to a Colchester depot: but they also reached Silchester, Cirencester, Lincoln, Wroxeter and Richborough. Bath stone fared as far afield as Colchester; Purbeck marble is found in Silchester and St. Albans; West Riding stone and roofing-slates went to East Yorkshire. Stamped flue-tiles and roof-tiles were ubiquitous, though distribution tended to be closely localised. Samian ware, to be found in the humblest villages, was normally imported from Gaul, but for a shorter period was also made in local kilns at Colchester, Pulborough and York. Coarse wares made in local kilns were distributed extensively in their regions and very widely in military districts : but certain classes of special wares, like the mixing-bowls (*mortaria*) stamped with their makers' names, were traded for long distances all over the province.

No less important was the development of shipping, especially for heavy goods in bulk. Here the aids to official shipping, such as harbours, quays and lighthouses, were also of service to merchants. Wine and oil have already been mentioned as constituting an important item among bulk imports. Direct sea-trade between York and Bordeaux was concerned in such produce. Huge pottery consignments, weighty yet fragile, came from overseas, shipped from the Gallic Channel ports or the mouth of the Rhine : and the wreck of such a cargo of late second-century Samian ware gave a name to Pudding Pan Rock, near Whitstable. Metal goods in earlier days and glass table-wares later also formed important bulk imports. The special interest of the military in shipping for supplies and troop transport is attested by the choice of navigable rivers for the sites of all three permanent legionary fortresses and of many forts, manifestly with a view to easing the burden upon the roads : and maritime stores-depots, at Richborough in the first century and at South Shields in the third, though there must also have been many others, demonstrate the vital part played by sea transport in commissariat organisation.

But despite the relative ease of importation, development of provincial resources was vast. One of the outstanding activities was mining for silver, separated from lead by cupellation, in the Mendips, Shropshire, Flintshire, Derbyshire, Yorkshire West Riding and Northumberland. To which must be added gold from Caermarthenshire and copper principally from Anglesea. Many of these mines were State undertakings, worked by slaves or criminals and supervised by the military, and the silver-mining yielded ingots or pigs of its by-product, lead, stamped with the Emperor's name. Private lessees of this State property are, however, known for both lead and copper mines. Iron-mining, of which the organisation in Britain is unknown, was undertaken on a large scale in the Weald and Forest of Dean, while small fields of ore were developed all over the country, as, for example, in Lincolnshire and Northumberland. Indeed, small-scale development of local resources was a feature of Romano-British economics, and may be regarded as natural to an age of limited possibilities of transport. Local development is well seen in the exploitation of coal, extensively sought in local outcrops, notably in Somersetshire, South Wales, South Yorkshire, Lancashire, Northumberland and Stirlingshire, and used for domestic and industrial fuel.

Less spectacular than mining, but more important, was the steady development of the countryside, resulting from the requirement that the province should feed itself and its garrison with corn. Corn was the Roman army's staple food, which the province was bound to provide by the first terms of settlement ; and the development of corn-growing involved must have been materially assisted by the good iron tools now available and encouraged by an expanding market. The heavy plough, a Central European invention introduced to Britain on a limited scale and in a limited area before the Roman conquest, certainly owed its general distribution to the Roman peace. Clearing of lighter woodland now began. But the most spectacular phase of Romano-British agriculture is unquestionably the exploitation of the marshy Witham valley and the adjacent Fenland by surface draining and great catchwater-drains, such as the Car Dyke and Reach Lode in Cambridgeshire or the much vaster Car Dyke and Foss Dyke in Lincolnshire. The surface drainage was a typically Roman development, derived from the Mediterranean exploitation of alluvial marsh-lands, and was probably more widespread in Britain than is at present realised : a recent discovery attests its use in Saltney Marsh, near Chester, while air-photography has shown that large areas of the Fenland were thus reclaimed

TRAGIC MASK, IN IVORY
Probably second century A.D.   Found at Caerleon, Monmouthshire

for rich and profitable agriculture. The catchwater-drains in the Lincoln-shire area lent themselves to use as canals for barge-traffic, whereby the Fens were placed in direct communication with York, the seat of the Northern Command, and a proportion of their produce may thus have gone to feed the army. But corn is not the only crop which the Fens may have grown. Flax and linen production, for example, could have come into the picture. It is none the less clear that a great military market, with its many opportunities for large contractors and small traders, was a great fillip to adjacent areas. The villas of East Yorkshire or the South Wales coast plain, small but highly comfortable farm-dwellings, witness the steady prosperity of the hinterland of the Northern and Western military zones, and the recent discovery of a villa close to Durham City provides evidence, supported in other directions, of developed farming in the very heart of the military zones where good land offered. This steady and unexciting development was one of the most important consequences of Roman peace and the best possible contribution to the economic prosperity of the province.

Market-gardening also had no doubt an important part to play in local economy, especially near the urban centres and the military concentrations. This and fruit-growing were spheres in which the Britons had much to learn from the Roman world, for the improvement of varieties had long been one of the deep and profitable interests of the wealthy Roman estate owner. That the vine had already been introduced may be suspected from the proud display of the vine-leaf on the British coinage of the Sussex area in rivalry with the corn-ear of Cunobellinus in Essex. But viticulture was an art much studied and elaborated by Roman hands, and vine-stems are associated with at least one Romano-British country estate, at Boxmoor in Hertfordshire.

Another valuable native industry was the wool trade. The temperate climate of Britain made its pastures valuable, and the Downs and similar open pastures underwent considerable development as sheep-walks for wool-production. British woollen cloaks take a good place in Diocletian's price-controls for the Eastern Empire. Estates at Darenth in Kent, Titsey in Surrey and Chedworth in Gloucester, in the sheep-raising Downs or Cotswolds, contain large fulling establishments for whitening cloth, in each case larger than local needs could demand. This points to a development of estate industries comparable with that of the Moselle region, where cloth production and export in Roman times are portrayed on carved reliefs from great funeral monuments such as have not survived in Britain. The trade was sufficiently large and stable for official development. An Imperial weaving-shed, almost certainly slave-run, was established in *Venta*, presumably pasture-girt *Venta Belgarum* (Winchester), to produce cloth for the Services. The kindred industry of dyeing, part of which was centred in Silchester, also deserves notice, this being one of the rare cases where we can attach a specific industry to a tribal capital. It is not difficult to picture the finished cloth from the downland home establishments of the Atrebates being brought into town for dyeing and distribution.

One of the results of this developing enterprise—industrialisation we can hardly call it—must have been an important increase in the artisan class. There were so many new trades that employment must have been expanding and population on the increase. But much artisan labour was performed by slaves rather than free men, and the effect of slave labour upon population was crude restriction rather than untrammelled increase. There was little room for children in a slave-run establishment : and the numerous infant burials associated with almost every kind of dwelling, and in particular with country estates, is to be interpreted as imposed infanticide rather than as a high infant mortality due to natural causes. The existence of building labour in large bodies which could be officially directed to work elsewhere is appositely illustrated by the transfer of such labour, of which the British province had a surplus, to repair public buildings of the Gallic towns at the opening of the fourth century. But guild membership as a basis of call-up is here more likely than slave labour.

Yet growth in local industries must have been large, whatever the conditions of control. The potteries at Castor on Nene (*Durobrivae*), which extended for miles along the river bank and of which the owners lived in comfortable houses among the clay-pits, must have employed large numbers of workers in the production of their elegant vessels, mostly drinking cups. At Crambeck in East Yorkshire, which supplied a military market covering a great part of the North, the houses are mere shacks and the industry was evidently organised upon different lines. And a low but interesting stage of organisation is represented by the New Forest potteries, run by semi-itinerant workers, who exhausted a pocket of clay or woodland and then moved on to other sites, disposing of their wares between-whiles. Tileries, on the other hand, with owners' names or initials stamped on their products, may be expected to have been slave-run and more stationary. Their heavy products tended to be strictly regional in distribution. Some were State-owned or worked by corporations, and in the military area soldiers made their own bricks and tiles locally.

The manufacture of small objects in the Kimmeridge shale of Purbeck, Dorsetshire, well known in earlier ages, was developed into the production of trays and platters, veneering, furniture and elaborate lathe-turned objects. The substance was valued the more because it was deemed to have magical protective qualities. Whitby jet, similarly esteemed, was worked into jewellery and fancy goods, such as distaffs and hair-pins, with the highest skill ; and the finished articles seem to have been widely distributed throughout Britain and exported to the Rhineland.

Natural products must also be mentioned. Oysters abound in Britain, and were evidently specially enjoyed by the soldiery, outside whose forts oyster-shell deposits are so large and so common as to mark the oyster as the equivalent of the modern fried fish. Pearls were obviously not the object of such oyster breeding, but British pearls were collected from the shores and ranked by Roman jewellers as second-class. British hunting-dogs, on the other hand, took an important place. Among the breeds can be recognised a wolf-hound, while Claudian refers to bull-dogs and Oppian to a sort of pointer.

Finally, there is interesting evidence of trade with the outlands beyond the Imperial frontier. Discoveries on Scottish native sites of wine-jars, pottery and objects of bronze and iron, particularly tools, indicate a considerable and steady volume of trade touching all the coast-lands of East and West and the brochs of the far North. The first stages of such a voyage, and hopes of profit, are indicated in the dedication in verse by a now name-less trafficker found at Bowness-on-Solway : "grant that the profits of my enterprise may add good faith to my vows, and I will later sanctify my poem with gilded letters one by one." The goods acquired by such traders in exchange for their wares were principally rare and valuable furs, skins of seals or bears, walrus tusks, pearls, or caledonian bears for the circus or amphitheatre, cattle, ponies and slaves. Irish trade was much slighter, if regular at all, to judge from the very limited number of Roman finds there recorded.

Taken at large, the picture of Romano-British economy is an interesting one. It was no barter-economy. An abundance of current coin everywhere indicates the general use of coin of all denominations, and the need for small change is illustrated by local issues of bronze or silver-washed coinage and by forgeries. The cantonal capitals or tribal centres are, so far as we know them, well equipped with shops, and were clearly local distribution-centres of some importance. Slave labour and the concentration of wealth in landed estate tended to keep manufacturing installations small and localised, and it is clear that many sides of industry were based upon country estates rather than towns. But this evidence does not cover the largest and most prosperous towns, and may therefore be misleading. So far as it goes, however, it supports the conclusion based upon a study of the town-plans which we possess, that in many of the British tribal divisions wealth and enterprise were concentrated in the country rather than in the towns, and that the town served as an administrative centre and a retail market rather than to concentrate wealth or attract a populace engaged in wholesale manufacture.

BRONZE PATERA OR ARMY MESS-TIN
First century A.D. Found at Glyn Dyfrdwy, Denbighshire

THE CAUSES OF COLLAPSE

TO those who would trouble to read it, the history of the province of Britain furnished a series of lessons on risks and calamities likely to attend certain courses of action. The first of these lessons was the danger of participation in civil war within the Empire, usually caused by ambition in a provincial governor-general. The founder of the Empire, in creating the system by which the great Imperial provinces were governed, had safeguarded himself against revolts on the part of governors by establishing a dual control. The army was commanded by the legate, or governor, while finance and taxation were the affair of a procurator, or Imperial Treasury agent. This system carried Britain safely through the Civil War of 69-70, when other provincial armies were making the dangerous discovery that "Emperors could be made elsewhere than in Rome." But it was not proof against the crisis of 193-197, which followed the assassination of Commodus and left the succession in dispute between nominees of the Guards and the legions.

After Severus, governor of Pannonia, had been declared Emperor by his legionaries, he had astutely eliminated Albinus, the governor of Britain, by offering him the position of Caesar or heir-apparent. But Albinus presently made a bid for supreme power, crossed to the Continent with all troops he could muster and, risking all, lost all in a great battle near Lyons, in February 197. On the news of this shattering disintegration of the provincial army the Northern barbarians invaded and devastated the empty military zone before the government of Severus could control the situation. A false step by its governor thus cost the province an immense fortune in blood and treasure : and the price paid to the interests of central government was the division of the province into two, in order to curb the power of future governors, and a consequent rise in the cost of provincial administration.

The second lesson concerned the folly of separatism. In 287, Carausius, admiral of the Channel fleet at Boulogne, had come under suspicion of self-enrichment during the suppression of piracy and even of collusion with pirates. To avoid execution, he transferred his fleet and power to Britain, proclaimed himself Augustus and reasserted his power in Northern Gaul with British backing until 293, when he was driven off the Continent and soon murdered by his chief Treasury official, Allectus. Three years later Britain was reunited to the Empire by Constantius I, but only at the expense of a severe defeat of the provincial army loyal to Allectus. These events not only brought down upon the military zone a northern invasion as severe as the last, but plunged the civil province into a confusion which almost involved the sack of London itself. As a sequel, Britain had also to accept further subdivision and multiplication of senior bureaucratic posts. The two provinces now became four.

The third lesson was the vulnerability of the province to attack by sea. By the close of the third century, the weakness of the central government, torn between Continental usurper-Emperors and palace or army conspiracies, had exposed the Western provinces to extensive raiding by barbarians bent on pillage. Britain, either profiting by past lessons or suitably weakened by partition, had been tolerably free from revolt and civil strife. But the initiative of the provincial government must have been gravely weakened by the central instability. Governors could take no action against new dangers without sanction from a central administration often too weak or too preoccupied to give attention. Thus, while some temporary measures had been taken, like the fortification of Richborough, it was not until the new autocracy of the fourth century had been established by Diocletian and his colleagues that South-Eastern Britain was provided with systematic coast-patrols by sea and land under a Count of the Saxon Shore. This system, improved as time went on, secured the province from its most aggressive overseas raiders : but, while isolated information is here and there available, it is not clear whether any developed system was established upon other coasts to meet raids from Ireland, whence the Scotti were beginning to descend upon the province, and from Scotland beyond the Grampians, whence Picts were indulging in vindictive and savage sea-raids. In such a state of knowledge generalisation is dangerous : but there is general agreement that the new measures were adequate to ensure the peace and prosperity of the province until after the middle of the fourth century. Then occurred an unprecedented event, which eloquently attests the efficacy of the previous countermeasures. The barbarians, Saxons, Franks, Picts and Scots, combined to achieve by concerted action what they could not contrive in small units, and to sack the province by a co-ordinated assault. The Count of the Saxon Shore, in charge of coast defence, went down fighting, and the Duke of the British provinces, in command of the field force, was ambushed following treachery and desertion by the garrison of the northern frontier. Robber and pirate bands reached the very walls of London itself. This invasion was a heavier blow than had ever before fallen, and cannot be dissociated from the sweeping changes which had by now taken place in the provincial army.

Until the middle of the second century, the Roman provincial garrisons of legionaries and auxiliaries had been composed of units originally raised outside the province which they occupied; and, although there was some local recruitment, it was a general principle to replenish by drafts from

DEVOLUTION OF THE COINAGE
Fifth century A.D. 'minimissimi,' compared with an English halfpenny

44

THE RELIEF OF LONDON BY COMBINED OPERATIONS
A.D. 296. Gold medallion of Constantius I, from Arras, France

abroad though not necessarily from the home country of the unit to which they were posted. But local recruitment tended to increase as regiments attained settled stations, and new sources of man-power also included extensive drafts from aggressive frontier tribes which were conquered but not absorbed within the Empire. Ex-servicemen from such units were settled on the land, there to rear families whose sons could become soldiers.

Still more important developments occurred in the third century. After 212, legionaries were no longer distinguished from auxiliary troops by possession of the citizenship, except in the case of drafts from the outlands, since all free-born provincials became Roman citizens. Serving legionaries received the right to lease land, and the privilege, with hereditary service attached, was soon extended to the auxiliary regiments. Local recruitment allied to land tenure became an established practice and by the fourth century it had become a regulation that frontier regiments comprised either local recruits or barbarian drafts obtained by treaty from outside the Empire, and that they were settled upon the lands which they defended, with military service as a hereditary obligation. The way was then prepared for the splitting-up of the legions into small units and the creation of field-forces and frontier forces, in a wholly new organisation. Only the names of the older units survived, half disguising on paper the fundamental changes which had taken place.

Frontier troops were thus now of totally different composition from their predecessors of two centuries before. They comprised either local recruits or barbarians, and even the local provincial recruits might tend upon occasion to make common cause with the tribes beyond the frontier rather than with the administration inside it. The only course open to a province isolated by separatism or barbarian raiding, or drained of its own youth by

45

disaster, was to hire mercenaries whose loyalty was doubtful in the best conditions. Thus, in the late fourth century the condition of the army made obedience to the lessons of history even more imperative than before if the stability of the British provinces was to be maintained. Three requirements stood out as fundamental. The locally recruited armies must not be risked in Continental adventures : separatism must be avoided : touch must be maintained with the central administration. Yet in fact each of these conditions was repeatedly broken. In 383 Magnus Maximus plunged into a bid for power on the Continent and five years later had lost the flower of the British army at Aquileia. The same thing was attempted again in 407 by the usurper Constantine III, when the island had been cut off from the central government by the great barbarian inroad into Gaul. Presently, in 410, came the well-known instruction of Honorius to the British urban communities to provide for themselves.

The inherent weakness of the social and economic structure of the province was now revealed. The ingrained habit of the local aristocracy to shun town life and to concentrate upon their estates may well be considered to have proved of value in the fourth century, when towns tended to be considered as administrative units and markets only, while the growing burdens of taxation in money and kind depended more than ever upon prosperous country estates. Taxation in kind was developed in the later third century out of the earlier army-levies in the face of a collapsing currency due to depreciation. Prices and values never regained sufficient stability to abolish it, and an indirect consequence was the official marking of many finer metal objects with their bullion value, to make them payable or realisable as levies or taxation. In these circumstances, the estate productive of real wealth was the most valuable asset in the community. But the estate as a unit was clearly ill adapted to survive in an unsettled countryside. Not that the destruction happened rapidly, or that the results were immediately irretrievable. Nothing illustrates the recuperative power of the countryside better than the fact that St. Patrick, carried off by Irish raiders about the beginning of the fifth century, could return home many years later and find his family safe and sound. The devastation was in fact piecemeal, directed against a province already so subdivided as to be liable to break up in regionalism. One such region was clearly centred in Yorkshire, where the coins in the signal-stations, established after the invasion of 367-369, continue until the close of the century and may well have remained current for a little while after that. This was also so in the fort at Malton, which was the hub of the system, and in some adjacent farms which remained comfortable and prosperous for at least as long. The first hint of a changing situation is given by the presence, at the very gates of York, of an Anglian cemetery of early fifth-century type, suggesting not so much the collapse of the Romano-British community as a settlement of Saxon mercenaries. Excavations at Elmswell, near Driffield, revealing early

46

SILVER DISH WITH BACCHIC DANCERS
Fourth century A.D. From a collection of family plate, found at Mildenhall, Suffolk

Anglian and late-Roman or sub-Roman remains in the closest association, suggest the same thing: that in East Yorkshire Anglian mercenaries were called in and settled on the land which they were to defend, in the manner now traditional for some two centuries. The move must be connected with another event further north, the transfer of the allied Votadini under Cunedda to North Wales to drive out Irish settlers. But it implies a central power in York vigorous enough to arrange such matters and to pay for them in money, food and lands. Only when the community could or would no longer furnish the necessary pay and keep did the mercenary become the master.

This northern series of events, chronicled by archaeology rather than by history, is an anticipation or repetition—we cannot exactly date it—of the story of Hengist and Horsa in Kent, after 449. Until then, South-East

47

Britain was so full of sub-Roman influences as strongly to support the view that official connexions were established anew after 417, even to the extent of sending some field-troops. But by 427, when Bishop Germanus of Auxerre paid his first visit to quell heresy at Verulamium, government seems to have devolved upon the tribal communities and barbarian raiding was rife. Yet Verulamium was still intact and still ready to be engrossed in theological questions twenty years later when the second visit of the bishop was paid.

A remarkable illustration of the general devolution now taking place is provided by the coinage. Gold coinage, if continued, has not survived from this transitional age. But the silver coinage of the late fourth century lasted, worn and clipped, for at least a generation on the most conservative estimate, no doubt serving as the principal medium of valuable exchange. The bronze coinage, money of everyday account, devolved by stages. First came local imitations of the small-scale Roman coinage of the House of Theodosius. Then follow halved and quartered pieces of these denominations, representing economy in raw material rather than change in face value. Finally come the small minims, in three diameters from 7.5 to 2.5 millimetres, the last so small that it takes more than fifty to cover a halfpenny piece. These changes would be incomprehensible and inacceptable to Saxon immigrants or mercenaries. They must cover some decades and must be related to the needs of the local sub-Roman population. The coinage has so far been noted in Southern Britain from the Thames basin to the lower Severn. It is a valuable indication of continuing commerce and of regard for ways learnt from Rome. But it is also eloquent of the dearth of raw materials and the complete breakdown of the wider provincial control which would have made them available. It implies that all central authority was gone and that effective inter-regional commercial activity no longer existed. This is the atmosphere of civil war among British *tyranni*, self-made usurpers, and of the Saxon advances following the middle of the fifth century. The organised life of the Roman world had vanished in a tide of individualism and immigration.

SHORT BIBLIOGRAPHY

The Romanization of Roman Britain by F. Haverfield. 4th ed. 1923, Clarendon Press. —*Roman Britain* by R. G. Collingwood. 1923, Clarendon Press.—*The Roman Occupation of Britain* by F. Haverfield and Sir George Macdonald. 1924, Clarendon Press.— *The Archaeology of Roman Britain* by R. G. Collingwood. 1930, Methuen.—*The Roman Wall in Scotland* by Sir George Macdonald. 1934, Clarendon Press.—*Handbook to the Roman Wall* by Dr. Collingwood Bruce. 10th ed. 1947 (ed. I. A. Richmond), Andrew Reid, Newcastle upon Tyne